REFUSE

D1413996

PITT POETRY SERIES

ED OCHESTER, Editor

REFUSE

JULIAN RANDALL

UNIVERSITY OF PITTSBURGH PRESS

THIS BOOK IS THE WINNER OF THE 2017 CAVE CANEM POETRY PRIZE, SELECTED BY VIEVEE FRANCIS.

Founded in 1996 by poets Toi Derricotte and Cornelius Eady, Cave Canem is a home for the many voices of African American poetry and is committed to cultivating the artistic and professional growth of African American poets.

Established in 1999, the Cave Canem Poetry Prize is awarded annually to an exceptional manuscript by an African American poet who has not yet published a full-length book of poems.

Support for the Cave Canem Poetry Prize has been provided, in part, from The Ford Foundation, Lannan Foundation, and individual donors.

Published by the University of Pittsburgh Press, Pittsburgh, Pa., 15260
Manufactured in the United States of America
Printed on acid-free paper
10 9 8 7 6 5 4 3 2 1

ISBN 13: 978-0-8229-6560-2

Cover art: Jeff Manning, *Manifest II*. www.jeffmanningart.com
Cover design: Alex Wolfe

. . . either I'm nobody or I'm a nation

▪ DEREK WALCOTT ▪

CONTENTS

ICARUS ~~IMPOSTER SYNDROME~~

How much time do you really need me to spend on the lust
for an eternal summer   or a father's gaze   before I can say
Every flight makes me a little more dead and you can take it
on faith or at least the reasonable suspension of disbelief?
Which   I've been told   is the prerequisite of all good
myths   Do you believe me if I say that all I was ever good
for was a death   that was remarkable   only where
ambition gives way to a popular moral?   I am saying
it is a good myth   because so many hands keep painting it
this *good kid*   to whom   *this could have never happened*
if the world was not the world   This smart kid who only
ever lived   the once   and soon   or already never again
I am saying it is a good myth because we burn all the time
and at different velocities and this is how I first knew that
I was different   I was given an impression of what I could
never hope to operate   I was given the fable and never
left the ground   If I say that this is a story that ends
in drowning I think you know who must have given the eulogy
off camera   If this is the case I think you do not understand
the physics of ambition   when ambition is the only reason
that you are something like free   I mean from that height
you cannot enter the water   the heat has met your back
and if you hit the water   the ocean's desire to reject the living
would snap Icarus' neck before taking the *good kid* into the inevitable
Everything a father does to keep a son alive is a futile exercise
In certain iterations of the legend   Icarus must have been as dark
as me by the time he was what he was always going to become
And it is I think always the way with such things   For the longest
time I could not make it out of a poem alive   This one is no different
I was   conceived as a fable   It is always the way of such things
that I lift my tongue towards my mother's country and find the ridges
at the top of my mouth scalding   perdóname *I repent for not being*
enough of anything That I was placed in a school   like my own dark

father   miles from any reflection   until the river the lake the ocean
beckoned below   That I could hear doom sizzling at the back of my neck
for years before I realized what I want so much to make you believe
Every desire kills us by degrees Do you believe me if I say I only ever wanted
to be worthy of my father's grief? Of the kind of obsession that nearly drowns
us? Do I need to tell you that I am my father's son for you to know only one of us
can survive? How much do I need to tell you about how *a good son dies too*
before I can make you believe Daedalus circled until his throat was as raw
as any featherless bird?

REFUSE

A THOUSAND CARDINALS

Imagine my first moon
wasn't a moon at all
but a crescent incision
in my mother   Imagine
my disappointment
when I realized no light
would ever be so full
as the gore I passed through
just to be born

If I am ever as successful
                        at leaving as I aspire to be
I suppose it would go like this
        I decide to stay   and then a bloom
                                        of cardinals peel themselves
from my back   I splinter into a thousand dead
                                        relatives
just like that   I'm my mother's son   all over again

What was the last thing you loved enough
to open something that was not a border
I was born and the scar makes my mother
exactly the island that her parents fled

Every sacrifice begets a question
                    What would you give to never have to flee again?

I mean   my father asked my mother to not teach me Spanish
So I would not be *confused*   my mother traded her tongue
and I sound as if I am only his son   What sacrifice   to say allegiance
to my small dark mouth   and not be understood   on purpose
wash the moon   clean of crimson   until I was barely born at all

In order for me to exist   somebody has to have had sex
In order for me to exist   one thing has to be at the gate
                                        rattling   until answer
At the end of sex a sacrifice has to be made unless a sacrifice was made during
I do both   just to be safe   I give and give my tongue
                                        and I am my mother's son
because the tongue keeps showing up in my mouth

I want to stop   being   this way   I ask
what it would take to be a sacrifice worthy of the sacrifices that precede me
a trail of wings through which the sun appears to always be in retreat
I am placed in a school that costs my parents so much
The nature of sacrifice is recursive   we give up
home after home   a child is left at the brink
of what is known   and we trust an illogical love   that I could bring myself back
I want to know when enough has been given I want to know when I'm allowed
to stop

I ask my birth   to forgive me   when I cannot ask my mother
I leave a child   at the edge of my mouth   dare anyone *Wash the moon
clean of the child*   and this too is sacrifice and lineage   this too an incision
that made me possible

There's the kind of person who gives their life   for something
There's the kind of person who gives their life   to prove there was a life

Despite my best efforts   I keep growing back

Suppose to wash my mother clean   I freed my tongue
                                   of my own teeth
and nearly leapt in front of a train   to save my parents the shame
of knowing I am not as strong as my father   Suppose my mother called
right before   as I worked my knees loose from old transgressions to jump
Suppose only sacrifice staves off sacrifice   What other love is there
Suppose   the alternate ending   the train curves a long moon
I split   I bouquet   I stay   a thousand stains   a thousand cardinals

BIRACIAL GHAZAL: WHY EVERYTHING ENDS IN BLOOD

And what language exists with no word for blood?
What gets across the legend as quickly as blood?

Where I am from there are no words for my shade
Only nicknames   approximations for the blood

Blacktino   Lanegro   Halfbreed   Mutt   Progress
confused   a turmoil of skin   bouquet of hunted blood

I am a burden in every mouth   my name a minefield
people forget what I am exactly   but I end in blood

Two tone sacrament   Where the soil meets the sky
but never the horizon   child with the invisible blood

Like a sunset I am considered most beautiful when
I am disappearing   stitching a gown of my blood

Child with too many tongues   gone twice over
aftermath   a failed experiment of the blood

People ask *what are you* and I have no house
I bite my tongue into copper   search my blood

For a key   for a name that is not a translation for
Once there was a war here is what we did with the blood

THIS LAND IS WHERE WE BURIED EVERYTHING THAT CAME BEFORE YOU: AFRICAN AMERICAN HISTORY AND CONCEPTS OF OWNERSHIP IN EARLY ELEMENTARY EDUCATION

ABSTRACT:

Within the history of Afro-American existence much scholastic importance has been attributed to the weight of February. This is certainly understandable as Blackness in the pedagogical tradition is nothing if not a silhouette in a pelagic winter. However, understated in all of this is the significance of the "Token" as a kind of tragic hero in the tradition of sole survivors such as Odysseus. More specifically, how a boy might see his undoing and howl across the unflinching snow and never identify the echo. This Sonics of Blackness is a criminally under represented element of how one conveys to a room full of second graders the savage lick of a whip as a means of explaining an entire history. The question of this poem then is how the educator of the classroom approaches the subject of slavery when only one Black child sits in the room worrying at a shoelace, as if preparing. This poem takes as its primary subject a boy no older than 7 embraced by his white best friend as the white best friend states "I am glad slavery is over, I would have hated to own you." Followed by the boy sitting on his hands until they are blood bulbous and no longer entirely his own. How he looks beyond the window onto the playground and beneath the snow imagines an entire country; beneath that country, another.

FRIDAY NIGHT LIGHTS #1

Home field sits beneath six obnoxious moons so you know this is another planet. There's a field in Idaho where sparrows snap their necks by a combination of desire and proximity. This might be hearsay, but I believe it. The field in Idaho is blue, not the shade of anything you could drown in, but like Blue food coloring, which you can drown in if you try hard enough. All this to say, there's a football field in Idaho where I heard there's a man whose entire job is to sweep up little foolish deaths. Their field is not my field, but their death might be my desire. By nightfall there's so much light, there's barely a sky at all, I love it best this way. If you think I'm the bird in this scenario, you're right. Note my desperate not-wings, featherless and stark against the not-emerald. The grass is not grass but if you bow, and you will, your knees ache the same. At the edge of the field there's a school, at the edge of the school there's a me. In the road between the two I'm barely visible, a feather troubling a lake. Minnesota is full of lakes, Minnesota is full of cabins, Minnesota is full of lakes whose guts run thick with iron, Minnesota is full of things the light doesn't have the strength to reach. I lead with my head; I feel my neck warn me. Down the middle of me vertebrae groan into a range of hills the breeze cannot climb. My palms ripped clean of their soft by the iron of an iron bar, fished from a lake by the beak of a machine. I sympathize with the birds, I mistake things for home all the time. I do not look back; I dive into the boy

reckless for this land
I lower my crown   swear
I will die the king of something

IN A RARE MOMENT OF NOSTALGIA MY FATHER REFLECTS ON OBAMA'S FIRST INAUGURATION

*I don't want to start with the bullet or how you wanted to be president
because he was or how in my dreams I can watch the wind surge clean
from one side of your skull to the other or how I never wanted you to be
president or how hope is its own kind of plague or trepanning or how
round rooms make your mother dizzy or how often you forget she has
her own knuckles or how trepanning means carving a door in the skull
or entrances or broken windows or blood or how much white men hope
a well-placed wound can solve or how nobody brings you to god or how
only your mother goes to church or how she gripped her knuckles to
marble praying or how when he got out of the car your mother clutched
my shoulder into a string of bruises or how you have her face or how
the skull is a round room or how he got out the car or hope or how I hid
the bruises because each of them wore your face   I am saying you
looked just like your mother when you were sixteen   you wanted to
be president   in my dreams   you are already outside the car   when
hope opens the wound   fills the whole round room with blood*

TAXONOMY REGARDING MY MOTHER

First Mirror • Love Song on Low Volume • Country Where They Shower Beneath the Moon • Spine of a Rosary • Prayer in One-Part Harmony • Lottery Woman • Dawn Trickling Through the Blinds • Nation of Mourning Palms • Island of Two Countries • Sciatica's Nervous Civil War • Child of a Rebellious Sea • Vitiligo's Ravenous Bleach • Country where the Night Bathes You Best • Baptism • My Ignored Phone Call • My Translator for the Dying • My Ignored Text Message • Fistful of White Flags • Abuelita's Pallbearer • Best Cook This Side of the Trujillo Regime • Candle in an Empty Cathedral • Silk Knuckles • Praying Hands • Moonlight Splintering My Father's Palm • Love in the Time of Reagan • Here

I THINK EVERYBODY HAS A YEAR THEY NEVER REALLY LEAVE

If song is the yolk of grief, then a year is not dissimilar to a bruise. I come from a thread of tragic men mourning other tragic men. There are men I cannot touch when I need to and all of them are related to me. I am saying that once I was small and this is how I learned my father was going to die someday.

We were in the parking lot outside of Blockbuster; it was raining because I remember it raining; because I am always ready to conjure something to hide my father's grief in. It must have been 2004 because every station was playing Dance with My Father on repeat. Luther Vandross had a stroke a month before and even the static wept. And there, to my left my father crying and my hands too small to fetch even a single tear.

He asked me a question that was not his question *Why does the music have to have words at all?* He means that to say the dead will only ever make them dead again. Outside the rain arced out; the widowed strands of a web, silver and perpetually falling. I wanted to strip the words from the air, let the piano repeat until grief exhausts itself. I know only a thin and selfish magic.

Beneath every mention of my father is the only truth he has ever wanted for me. He is going to die and my grief will be unremarkable. He is going to die and he told me so. He is going to die and this makes him not dissimilar to the constraints of a song. Every season dies eventually; this is what makes it a season. I ask too much, I return and return to this space before he could die. I hammer shrinking fists against my eyes, insistent, ugly as the fate of the rain.

SUMMER AFTER

After Gregory Pardlo

The summer after 4th grade
is the same summer I stumble
in on my father watching Purple Rain
for the first time   and I didn't know
who was on the TV   half as well
as I knew his voice   and I didn't know
any of the words   and I didn't know
my father could cry and I didn't know
then that my father had lost his job
and would not know for a year
But here   my father eager to hide
his salt beneath his massive hands
hands that are so much like a ship
that has been loved through a storm
or battle leather or anything shamed
by its own softness   until he is the man
I had always known while I ask him
        What are you watching?
he looks at me   and I am small
        when he responds
This boy lost his daddy too, but his daddy
taught him the music, now he's playing
to show his daddy how much he loves the music
And I didn't have the teeth then to say I was
sorry   I was defined by many openings
and still am   but I knew how to run
up the stairs and grab a stringless guitar
by its throat and run down the stairs
to strum air as I sat in his lap
and turned my face from him
so he could mouth all the words
perfectly

ELEGY FOR THE WINTER AFTER *TAINA* WAS CANCELLED

In the photograph   which never existed
I am roughly 7
on a block somewhere
near Michigan Ave

      It's worth noting that even
      in the photographs
      we have managed to save
      I look exactly like my mother
      save only the skin

We're outside of an FAO Schwarz
which was a place the other kids
at my school went to buy rocking horses
which cost hundreds of dollars

      It's worth noting that
      there is no word for the fear
      of waking up white
      though there are perhaps thousands
      for the fear of waking up with your mother's curses

Inside   white children are running   as wild as
white children   Bestial with joy
some of them looked like my best friend
some of their mothers looked like a woman
who got mad when I asked her to stop touching me

Lots of people assume my mother is white
that my father   like all Black men
lusts for white women as February lusts
for anything exposed   My mother
is actually Dominican   an immigrant's
daughter with vitiligo   The only way I know
what she used to look like   a small island
on the back of her calf

I had toys at home   but I wanted their toys
I don't want to be them   but I want what they have
This knowledge that there is always more of something
I aspired most to be a casual violence

                              and am still disappointed

I am lucky   to grieve most often what could never bleed
that the blood in my memories is almost always mine
I grieved Taina while I watched That's So Raven
If I knew anything before it was my time to know it
it is ~~how the static pricked my face to pull me closer~~
~~how there were so many white folk on the screen~~
~~how easy that sort of famine arrives~~
~~how scarcity runs the length of me~~
~~how a choice can cost me half my blood~~
~~how my mother gave up teaching me Spanish that winter~~
~~how scarcity runs the length of me~~
~~how scarcity runs the length of me~~
~~how scarcity runs the length of me~~

how there can only be one

In the photograph
which never existed
I massaged the frost
into a mirror
pressed my head too close
to the cold of FAO Schwarz
My face briefly superimposed
on the chaos and smile
think *It must be nice*
Before my mother dragged me away
and later that night
my father told me I need to stop
talking like a little white boy
And I stared at my hands
and sucked the ash off them
before I headed to my room
which was a good room
And thought of that other city
within my city   that window
so pristine it could be a TV
never burdened with static
wondered if the space I rubbed
to look through was still there
My own small brown face
a bruise in the glass

CHICAGO*

I am from Logan Square
in Illinois   there are tornadoes
In Chicago   the city breathes too hard
we make our own disasters
If anything though
I am from the backseat of a Megabus
natural born asterisk
every claim is hesitant
if the bricks cannot remember your face
I am from somewhere
that is not my somewhere anymore

If I know anything it is this
any good survival
tries not to be anywhere twice
I can only sleep on buses
in shoes I can run away in
so I may never be from anywhere again
The low hum of nowhere
constant as I ride past
a road so green
it might convince you
the world is not dying

WASN'T THE MINOTAUR BURIED HORNS FIRST: VULNERABILITY AND IDENTITY IN THE MYTHIC BODY

ABSTRACT:

Throughout the course of contemporary classic studies much scholarship has been done on the triumph of Theseus in his traversing of the labyrinth and his ill-fated sails. As a result, this poem is concerned with the symbolic significance of the lineage of the semi-bestial mythic body as a contemporary site of identity politics. Throughout this poem it can reasonably be assumed that some discussion of the symbolic barrier of placing a shameful beast inside a series of intraversible walls can stand as a place marker for a decidedly unpopulated and, it follows naturally, unmirrored existence. What can we, as citizens of the poem, learn from a son who has never seen his own face not caked in gore and other casualties of loneliness? In this vein, the poem eschews a beginning in the Aegean Sea in favor of an image of a Biracial child sitting in a lunchroom in Omaha, Nebraska being told by alabaster colored children, who could barely be troubled to acknowledge the beast otherwise, all the sports his blood will make him "a monster" at, and then the boy's fingers weeping scarlet onto the linoleum his skull freshly crowned with the beginnings of horns.

A POEM ABOUT TREES THAT ISN'T ACTUALLY A POEM ABOUT TREES

The thing is/my father is not/a saint/and never pretended/otherwise
the thing is/my father is black/and this is a poem/with trees/but nothing
dies/but not for lack of effort/the thing is that I don't remember/the fight
but it was a long time coming/in Omaha Nebraska/there were trees/I bled
and was outnumbered/and that is all I like to remember/the thing is/I don't
remember what we fought about/until my jaw clicks/I don't remember/how
many times my blood/was fast at 14/but this is a blush/I can remember/I hated
him/that day/that hour/his massive weight/which was a country/I could barely
pronounce/I was prostrate and swelling/my mother screamed/and never stopped
I ran/because that is my trade/because that was what my body was good for/in
Omaha and anywhere else/I am not very fast/only leaking crimson/at the edges
of my mouth/the thing is/that I do not know where I was going/I never do/my
jaw clicks and I know only/*not here/not here/not here*/the thing is that I hid in the
trees/the borders of where we were trying to leave/I pulsed/and cursed/the stars/
the thing is that my father only ever hit me/in Nebraska/for cursing/he drove
his fist/into my chest/and I couldn't breathe hard enough to cry/mercy is not an
heirloom/I swung wildly at the sky/then laid very still hoping not to be found/
praying he would not come/and my mother brought me back into the house/
pulled the twigs from my hair/pressed the steak to my swelling/everything until
my blood was even more unrecognizable/the thing is/that he said he was sorry
and I know that he was/the thing is that I did not forget/I never do/I remember
everything we can call a tradition/the thing is that I learned the trees could not
hide me/the thing is if I cannot hide there/it is just something I want to burn
down/I wanted everything/to know my raw/and shudder/at the steak's clumsy
kiss/to stare only into red/I wanted to fight I wanted to win/the thing is/I love my
father/I did not want to tell this story/but he bragged his victory to my sister/over
Christmas once/and my jaw still clicks/before a storm/he told me like all Black
children/*I brought you in/I will take you out/I will make another/just like you*
the thing is/that the night my father almost killed me/I learned my mother/had
a miscarriage before me/a boy/whose heart refused/to beat/his blood placid/
like a lake/he had no name I was already the replacement/and they loved me/and

still do/so much they sent me to camp to climb things/with children who looked nothing like me/divine love/to put me elsewhere and hope I would float/the thing is/I had camp the next morning/and my lip would not retreat we told everyone that I ran/into a tree/we blamed the trees/for what only a hand/could build

NEARLY 7 YEARS AFTER THE FACT A BOY WHOSE NOSE I NEARLY BROKE HITS ME UP FOR BRUNCH

I wasn't unprovoked
back on the 8th Grade DC trip
my mother was mentioned
& that is how I was christened
the other amongst others
I look like no one except her
they said *Your momma an illegal*
Your momma tongue is an elective
Your momma must have pulled you out
of the river   I was both of the shorelines

when I say   river[1]   I mean I cannot belong
to something I cannot drown in
I mean I resemble something
that also breaks bodies in defense
I mean sometimes being Biracial
is to have two half-filled glasses
& die of thirst anyway

---

1. This is less about the shame I have been willing to let neighbor my tongue all these years. Do I know who I am? More than I like to admit. I look like my mother, that's more than many people get. I looked so much like her then and she lived in Omaha, auctioning off my family's great sin, our desire for nicer things made her radial. Every morning of 8th grade I woke up in the same apartment as my father, beginning to understand our curse, our similarities, our gears with teeth in the same place. This scared us both and she was not there. She was not there and we fought. She was not there and I blamed her and hid my face beneath fitted hats that made me look more like my father's son, and only ever his son. The hats were cheap, they raised little cartographies of oil where my face becomes her hair. The other Black boys in the grade were afraid of me, the boy with the mother so far it made me foreign by association. They were so afraid I thought we could never be friends again. Everyone else was white, and so I say "I drowned in that year," though we lived in Chicago amid a bumper crop of wind. I could breathe just fine. But when she called and said the house was not ours anymore and neither was the money, for a moment and only a moment, I drowned in her absence.

IN THE NETFLIX TRAILER OBAMA SAYS "I DON'T FIT IN ANYWHERE" WHILE ANTHONY HAMILTON PULLS A BURNING CITY OUT OF HIS MOUTH

And the song is not about anything
in particular   just melody and wound
pain is true enough for a man to pass
for a whole country   And he is young
and named Barry then   And I think of
how my parents flinch sometimes when
I say my name   How it sits opaque
as a kidney stone   jagged sugars
a slow waltz with what is forbidden
Barry dances with white girls and glances
uncomfortably with all the Black boys
and we all know the white girl is a phase
a counterbalance to the basketball
which is either a very obtuse Atlas reference
or a reminder that Barry does Black stuff too
and I used to think wherever a white girl
could see me is where I was from
I did not say Love
I did say my name was David which is not untrue
and the song is throbbing by now
MySoulIsOnFireMySoulIsOnFireMySoulIsOnFire
David dances near the white girls and plays basketball
David hasn't sung since the last white girl he wanted
David   body of static   the electric glazing the TV
clingy and inconvenient down to the touch
the song is winding down now
scabbing over into an exhausted piano

Barry smokes a cigarette   David was never alive
Anthony Hamilton reaches into the back of his mouth
pries the gristle of a repossessed house from between
two molars and it is dark and neighbored with callouses
asks   *Is this where you're from?*
Barry says   *We are Americans*
I say   *yes*

OBAMA SAYS "MUTTS LIKE ME" IN THE MIRROR EVERY MORNING WHILE I GET READY FOR SCHOOL

Fog holds the mirror captive
one word splits the mirror
soft   a dragonfly's migration
dares to trouble the water

One word splits the mirror
a fracture no wider than a country
dares to trouble the water
his face wading in its own reflection

A fracture no wider than a country
a silvering hairline   wound in the glass
his face wading in its own reflection
the fracture is not vertical

a silvering hairline   wounds the glass
in this nation even what wants us doesn't
the fracture is not vertical
it's a failure in the design near the mouth

even what wants us doesn't
give me a mutt and I will know family
the mouth   a failure in the design
in the absence of my name

give me a mutt and I will know
each yellowed tooth
in the absence of my name
it is only ever a beast

I step loose from the shower
baptism is a tricky business
a small body skimming sacred
it's barely a miracle at all

This business of baptism
unbraids me
it's barely a miracle at all
how much I am like *them* is

unbraiding me
I am not biracial like he is
how much I am not like *them*
is a different map altogether

I am not his kind of biracial but
there are constants between us
a different map altogether
question of what is & what swells

A constant between us is desire
reflection is negligible geography
what is & what swells to chaos
I am such a little sin honestly

The negligible geography of
this body alone in the snow
Little sin at school I am called *Obama*
it is only ever my face

THE ACADEMY OF ACCEPTABLE LOSS

I'm new here and all I know about Minnesota is weather reports and weather reports. To say *there is snow here* is also to note that there is nowhere that the sun is not in the sky; made impossibly weak by distance and little collections of water condensing it down to grey light. They say there is Winter and Construction and if I'm a season, a little tapestry of months made kin by heat, I'm definitely Construction. I'm fifteen after all, what else could I be but scaffold on a building perpetually on the eve of becoming? A loose tooth atop a better bone, blood is at the root of all advancement. All the food tastes like copper. Wisdom teeth itch into being at the back of my soft mouth, the path to normalcy is a well-practiced wound. Something stirs beneath flesh, gags at my touch and this is how I grow older, fingering what will rot in isolation.

Let me make the stakes clear, there are only four Black boys in the photo including my own perpetually blurry face. The little country I put in the mirror always fraying in the steam. Out of all these Black boys I'm always referred to as *the smart one, Obama, Mr. President, Gorilla* taxonomy of everything but my own damn name. I have what one might call a difficult name if they have the kind of tongue that considers a name by proximity to their own. I hate substitute teachers with a mythic passion, in each roll call pause, a me. I exist in a space between letters, without me the whole thing is illegible. And this is my service, the brief architecture that the class giggles inside of. Somedays I correct them, and somedays the name is a casualty I leave smaller lives to pick clean. It's not that I don't care, I just know that I was put here to beat rich white people at a game they made up centuries ago and chess is predicated on acceptable loss.

Me, Mike, Medaria and Sammy make up one lunch table out of 30 and we are a loud country. All of us a parade of bulls in a kingdom of glass. Nobody sits here unless we mean them to, a seat at the table finally our shit to hand out or retain. There's a feast but it's enough to think we are letting them starve of our company and not the other way around. We live inside a pedagogy of plenty, families that own boats and cabins which have names that echo deeper than our own. We debate our own bodies or who finna act up in front of these white folk who pay our tuition and then not invite us to shit. Medaria textin his girl, while Sammy sits quiet as landscape, Mike lyin bout some girl he smashed in Paris and I'm dreaming us all a bigger table, a little heaven where we are nobody's silent. We all too young to be anything but a pastoral of finnas, quick shapes against the snow, teeth rattling in the cellar of a still young jaw. All the Black boys in this poem are still alive, one day you'll read that and it will never be true again.

It's February in Minnesota and ten thousand lakes give birth to ten thousand Narcissus. I mean the best thing you can be in Minnesota is a hockey player. I can't skate. Never even been on ice that you could skate on. In Chicago, we have Lake Michigan and walking across that gaudy tundra is how you fuck around and drown. Still, there is something in how a blade kisses an incision into the ice that I can only think of as desire. I mean the best thing you can be in Minnesota is a hockey player. It's so cold parts of me that are designed not to freeze, freeze anyway and it's all I can do to keep the ash at a manageable level of visibility. But what about Narcissus? What about each of the lakes that they call The Lake? What must it be like to have every move accompanied by a howl? What must it be like to flay the lake into applause, into suffocating noise? What must it be like to look at a mirror, expect white girls, and not fear death?

The teeth of our boots punch small archipelagos into the snow, there is a cavity for everywhere I've been until winter does its work again. What you can map into something profound about erasure I can only pronounce as Tuesday. I have no date to the dance and what's new about that really? I am neither rich nor white nor do I play hockey and so the white girls I'm lusting for think of me more as their favorite brick in a wall they lean against sometimes to gossip. I don't want them so much as I want what they have to offer. Out at the cabins people have sex, often. I watched Joey tease a girl for losing her virginity and she went so red I remembered that she had blood, so red she was a siren rouging the whole sky, so red I could never not see her again. I would like to be seen, for that I'd trade my virginity, for that I'd trade anything on my body.

Leaning against the collapsible wall at the party whose purpose I can't remember the other Black dude tells me he misses when *it was cool to be Black*. Late again to my own desire I sip my punch, nod, watch this little symphony unfold where I can watch people steal outside and just be grateful for the inescapable bass. Disturbia is playing in this culdesac and I think I'm thinking about football which I play now so that I can have a hoodie to give to a girl and a body beneath perpetually mid-flex, a little neighborhood of muscle with all the doors unlocked. I was kind of an asshole honestly. Anyway, other Black dude is still talking about some raw shit he got into last week with this girl from Wayzata who is now in the hallway making out with the white boy with the wet j from my school's basketball team. I don't really have a reason to be here, I don't have a reason to be anywhere. I curse the moon, not its distance, but for its audacity to return at all. I don't belong here, borrowing glimpses of a face under the colored glow, none of the light stays. The moon grows a fat white neon just beyond the window where a boy is now half clothed as if it is isn't like, two degrees outside. The moon is a better codeswitcher than I am, this all makes me irrationally upset.

I spend the whole summer in the weight room tearing little holes in everything my momma gave me. I might get to start on the football team this season and nobody wants to wear a JV anything. I want this so bad I tear my arms, I tear my knees, my quads in the pursuit of newer flesh and I believe it is worth it. I was born out of a wound, I come from a wound again and again. I work out in the same spot as the hockey players and they're dreaming of rings too. Locks spill out from the back of their scalps in a way the physics of my otherness can't conceive. It's a trend, the barely flood framing the neck, all around me golden tidal waves, all around me little ambitious disasters.

My favorite English teacher can't stop saying nigger. With it a tide of fleeting nervous gazes keep washing up on the doorstep of my face. I mean we are reading Huck Finn and me and Medaria sit next to each other pretending to take notes and be offended when really we are emailing each other in a thread where we have rap battles. We've gotten very good at this, exchanging one expectation for another. I should probably be paying attention but this book has nothing to do with me outside being a receptacle. Every glance begs *We are sorry, so sorry.* Guilt is a currency I'm wealthy in and this thought is enough to make racism kind of funny, kind of survivable. Above the tiles are painted to look like Dante's inferno and the whole room smells like tea. The room where nigger is said the most is also the place I feel most at home. The irony is not lost on me while I think that behind me there is a hall made up only of doors, some with locks, some knowing you wouldn't dare.

I sprained my ankle on the opening play of the homecoming game
and kept playing because it was the first time we won in three years
and coach said *nobody wants to kiss a loser.* My foot has swollen
to the point it barely fits in my dress shoe and the metaphor is
obvious from there. The next week I will tear my groin and refuse
to tell anybody because we're playing DeLasalle and I hate them for
thinking they're Blacker than me. But tonight, Paper Planes sends
gunshots into the dusty rafters that make up a sky, and it's true, *all I
want to do is take your money.* And I did. If my family has a trade,
this is it: The sacrifice of the body, the swallowing of coins in order
to enter what is sacred and make it briefly ours. The swelling of my
foot presses its urgency against the scaffold of my Dad's best shoes
and this means I cannot dance without also writhing in agony. I
lean against the wall where it is least soaked, play the radius, watch
the crowd sway on the one and the three in this sweaty gym. Desire
looks really ridiculous from this angle.

I become a stag, transfiguration worthy only of myths that actually
explain nothing. Stag means *the lonely beast,* his lonelier crowns a
rough velvet aspiring to rule like good forests do. Something near
my face makes me intraversible. King of the hum between antlers,
the breeze waltzes through my tangled scalp and is nobody's bride.
Vaseline buffed my palms to a dull shine. In that moment and ever
since I loved that school as much as anything that has played a part
in my dying. I don't know if I found out I was an exile before or after
most of us, I don't what anomaly I belong to. I know that there is a
distance from the sun where everything is a wick, I played the radius
in a years long winter, and briefly, was warm.

PREGAME PRAYER WITH COMPLETE CITATIONS

Our Father who art in Heaven[1]
Hallowed be thy name[2]
Thy Kingdom Come[3]
Thy will be done[4]
On Earth as it is in Heaven[5]
Give us this day[6]
Our daily bread[7]
And forgive us our trespasses[8]
As we forgive those who trespass against us[9]
And lead us not into temptation[10]
But deliver us from evil[11]
For thine is the kingdom[12]
The power[13]
The glory[14]
Amen[15]

---

1. My own father will miss pregame in the act of being a Good Son, of calling my grandmother who will accuse him of being a thief. For this small, repeated trespass, I briefly hate her. I ask you, bless his throat; that I might hear him as I cleave a boy loose from what he holds precious.

2. May the crowd have cause to say my name, may they find no humor in its mispronunciation, no confusion in its simple weight.

3. May the field be ours for all of October, may the Junior girls know a mosquito's lust. May the mosquitos fail; may I be that kind of impenetrable.

4. Spare me.

5. There is a cabin on a lake with a name I cannot pronounce. I know that is where the white girls take the white boys and learn how to be a boardroom or a family or just a carefree they interpret not at all carefree songs to be. This cabin is far Lord, it is far and I am not invited. This is the only heaven I can see. May I crack another boy's skull and in his defeat, find a key.

6. I know, I know this is the only time I pray. I promise what you know I will never deliver. Give me this day, tomorrow I will moan your name in a valley of ice and we can compromise, call that praise.

7. A boy wraps another boy in his arms and throws him towards the Earth. We call this "Eating," we are never full.

8. Mercy my knees, mercy my ankles, mercy my groin its little ravine west of want. Mercy what is already torn.

9. Forgive the fact that I will not forgive the invited intruder, forgive that I am willing to die for what I am only renting.

10. I do this as a means towards sin, you know that.

11. Spare me the purgatory of a sideline where I might have more to sacrifice but didn't. Spare me the agony of being the goat that survived.

12. There's no place on the field that the spiral of the chapel cannot be seen and yet, I have never seen it.

13. Grant me the strength to place fear in the space I used to be.

14. Grant me the acceptance of people who will never return my calls after this year.

15. Amen.

COVERAGE

And there   the boy's eyes meet mine
and this is how I know we must be enemies
October   and the air is full of mouths
a veil of mosquitos   smashing their bodies
against the stadium lights   and what I know
of desire starts here   watching their thirst
guide them to what cannot be drunk
I am 17   below their little convenient heaven
soft enough to penetrate   to slake what needs I can
and I want to break the boy in front of me
in a way we could mistake for romance   if not for
the pads   the lights   all the eyes we cannot see
but know are there   a body has purpose
mine cannot be seen   the body I mean

///

I play left tackle
my chest absorbs a parade of hands
I am good at being touched
in the name of protection
this waltz I do to say what little country is mine
I am too small to play at this kind of war
but I do what I have to to even the odds
My body belongs nowhere   so I claim his
&his &his   refer to them only by number

56: his gloved hand reached for my lips
        and found a fence
        so I shoved my hands into his ribs
        until I was his empty fingered god
8: long arms   basketball scholarship
    I press my everything into his back
    one of the only men I ever held

26: called me a faggot
    I took him at the knees
55: Tore my groin by a laying on of hands
    when I hold my lover   my hips moans his work

///

I also play linebacker
here my name sits ready
a stone ripening in the belly
of the lake upon which surely
there is a house which I am not
invited to   and this too
      is longing
there the athletic Black kids
drink with the rich white kids
half clothed in the lip of a boat
and this too demands my eyes
this too drives me sick with thirst

so I dress everything in my thunder
I lay down boy after boy on the field
and this is how I teach my presence
a pedagogy of desperation
I lord of this home I do not pay for
I lord of this body and its borrowed armor
I lord of a kingdom of inches
I crack a boy   out of this house
my cheek give way to the scarlet tang of pride
the chant gets the pronunciation just right
and this must be love
this chaos that blooms into my name

///

After the game we all draped in the thick stink of glory
undressed in our palace of chipped paint in a rich kid school
and what I know of desire   is a secret I keep from myself
a boy grabs at my dick   and calls me faggot for dodging
and this is how I know I am something like home
smiling in my boxers and stretching the scar tissue
of my rusted hip   &meeting nobody's eyes

YOU GOT MCDONALD'S MONEY?

"I don't even want you to look at nothing,
so you gotta go in there with your eyes closed."

■ BERNIE MAC ■

My father told me two things; a religion of sorts. *Don't eat these white folks' food when there's food in the house* and *Stop starving yourself, you making it look like I don't feed you.* And he did. For years I did not dream of empty, but chose it in the name of purity. I learned hunger and whiteness in the same place. I know how to refuse and not mean it; the only evidence a fist beneath the table, four half-moons sitting in my empty palm. Everything my mouth does is a sin, a windowless church swallowing the breeze. I drip *No thank you* by instinct; if I'm hungry, I'm nobody's child. If I never kissed the fingers of a foreign hand, I would have made for an exceedingly small casket. I still might.

FRIDAY NIGHT LIGHTS #20

His arm frayed just below
the skin   he had tried to bench press
250 pounds without warming up
everything has a limit   everything has a seam
I cursed his arrogance
the bar came down a slow guillotine
blunt the shade of moonlight
when something in him failed
I was a witness   when his pectoral tore
I was a witness   it was not sudden
the flesh separated from the flesh
he barely screamed
I had to drag him through the dust
on the stairs from the weight room
All the while he shouted *I'm pretty*
I'm fine I'm fine I'm fine I don't need
to go anywhere He thrashed in my arms
a new born   bird   featherless sputtering
and if I let him go he would have been free
the way we know free   wounded   lonely
sure that we would lose him
for the whole season
He got loose in the hallway of the school
we did not pay for   He ran the run of a beast
who is one arrow short of understanding
until he fell down in front of the admissions office
its glass door   its many white women
he lay there clutching his useless arm
telling me to go fuck myself   all of this still in front
of the admissions office   until I took him
by his shoulder   became something like a mother
if a mother can fear most their child
being exactly where they put them

if a mother can be like my mother
Medaria stop with this foolishness
white people are looking at you
in many ways these white women thought they were our mothers
I was afraid of that   there were only four Black boys in our grade
even as seniors   I feared a slow guillotine   the brief blade
of a white woman's smile   might have been the end of us
If every birth is an act of mercy
we lived within the most temporary country
we did not belong there   none of us
What greater mercy was there than to silence
the grief in its crib before it ended us all
White people are looking at you
Medaria got up   we walked to the trainer
All the while he mumbled like a sad radio
I'm fine I'm fine I'm fine I'm fine

FRIDAY NIGHT LIGHTS #51

During the away game against Delasalle Sammy dislocated his shoulder
and pushed it back into place without telling anyone. He collapsed five
plays later; something can be out of place and still be inside. When he
fell, he fell like a building, slowly and into himself until there is only
the quiet where a window used to be. There is a difference between
hurt and injured, something can be out of place and still be inside.
If we know anything it's that. Let me clarify what I mean by *we:*
when Sammy's shoulder buckled beneath his own desire the amount
of Black boys who were Seniors and had two working shoulders
decreased by 25%. Sammy failed the way a building fails, the rust's
appetite working its way through the walls of him. They took him to
the sideline; someone took his helmet off for him, someone brought
him water, someone asked him how much it hurt as if he wasn't going
to lie. Sammy didn't talk much, fuck he look like telling the truth
when we down by 14? I am not blameless here, I didn't think to hug
him then. I prayed that that would not be me. I prayed that what ails
me would be invisible enough to stay in. I tore my groin that game
trying to protect someone else. I tried to save somebody, I have not
walked the same since. Sammy cried for what felt like hours with the
game passing behind him, each thick braid spilling across his face.
The body is a building we had been inside our entire lives, somewhere
beneath Sammy one joint fumbled at the other in a way that could be
mistaken for lovers. But I said the body is a building so Sammy too was
a building; inside his arm one joint tried to fit into another, pulsing,
desperate as a sparrow making an exit with its skull.

THE SPOOK WHO SAT BY THE ONCE BOMBED CITY: PSYCHOLOGICAL EXPLORATIONS OF ANCESTRAL MEMORY THROUGH THE LENS OF RACIAL BATTLE TRAUMA

ABSTRACT:

In this poem we shall examine the figure of the "Token" as a doorway into a theory of ancestral memory; namely the collective consciousness of African American history. Thus, this poem is concerned with the question of whether what has been done can ever be undone; perhaps still more appropriately, whether what has been done has ever stopped happening? Concurrently, this is a poem that preoccupies itself with the question of what constitutes "the beginning" of ancestral memory? History implicates the hands, the ongoing question of whom they belong to; while a linguistic lens favors a tongue starved thin with retreat. For the purposes of this poem, let us favor the tongue. If we imagine ancestral memory as a museum with only entrances, then everything that has ever wished you dead might still be inside; thus the skull is a house filled with rusted knives. Where language intersects with all of this has fascinating physiological implications. Let us revisit the Token in college, attempting to say "No" and feeling dehydrated with the effort of it. If we presume the Token's college is near Philadelphia, he might learn about the MOVE Bombing and smell smoke everywhere. This matrix of possibilities lends itself well to the question of whether trauma and pain are inherent and, by extension, inherently linked. Simplified, the Token sits in his first Black studies course at the edge of understanding that Black Excellence is a failed form of teflon and rubs the exhausted tendons of his knees and wonders how long he has had to be faster than even the skin implies. He might answer "Always.," perhaps "Decades." Alternatively, he might have forgotten how to speak altogether.

THE SPACE BETWEEN SKINS IS CALLED A WOUND

So I guess that's my name now
I am progress
in the way a scab is progress
this is what it is to be biracial
conceived as a thin peace
the body's fragile truce
To each well intentioned finger
my body is just a precursor
to an unremarkable red

People ask *what are you?*
and my skin parts
eager to answer
what my mouth
can only rehearse
everyone falls in
curiosity killed the gaze

In this way I am something sinister
a shadow cast by a name
in the right light I am everything
I'm nobody's ideal horizon
I'm nobody's ideal
I'm nobody
or too much of everybody

I'm a kind of excess
a gold chain greedy for the light
a fat shiny river around the neck
in this way   I begin everywhere
and nowhere

I speak no Spanish
I mumble   every word
is a translation for exile

I make up for it
I throb near oceans
I speak inheritance fluently

TRANSLATION

My mother hangs up the phone
scrapes loose the tears
prepares to tell me
who is dying   this time

I speak no Spanish
my mother is the translator
of the dying
My family is always the dying
I say family despite the fact
I have attended none of their funerals

My abuelita was a ricocheting ghost
she died once   and I forgot
an entire language

Ok   I didn't forget
it just became inconvenient to remember
who wants a language for the living anyway?

An inventory of my tongue
yields nothing
that looks like my mother
the resemblance stops at the mouth

She is fluent in a language
I am only ever ugly in
She falls asleep in front of the TV
her show muted
I wonder if in her dreams
I can speak

ON THE NIGHT I CONSIDER COMING OUT TO MY PARENTS

I am afraid, of something I am, but have never named. My tongue is a refuge for secrets. How does one still fear banishment if they were born an exile? There's blood on the ground, no time remains so I'll lay it flat: I am Black and Dominican and Bisexual. There. If I die now, you'll have a hint for which god to petition. Sometimes, I look at a man and my hands are already digging into the small country of his back. In this way, the body is a distraction from what can make the body just a memory. My lips could bring a man's blood to the surface; my mother raised a curse and gave it her face. I am afraid to belong to another thing, to become still more no man's land. I am a trench; nobody comes to clear the dead. Somewhere, my mother is gripping a rosary to pray for men who look like me. Somewhere, my mother is praying for me. I do not want to give her something else to worry about. I am quiet, I bury no one, blood is drying beneath my nails, I do not know which me it belongs to.

(SELF) INFLICTED

I enter this story by the same door each time. Sweet tragedy, honeyed tongue of the night bucks down my throat again and again. It is as common a myth as I can bear: *Everyone Remembers Their First Time.* Suppose I do, for argument's sake. Suppose a memory knows violence inherently as a wolf knows that it deserves. Suppose we can call the result, result. That it is something more than my need to be sacrificed to myself. I did this to myself, the shots quivered, then didn't.

My face made smaller and smaller in the dimming melody. Taint me in the glass, eclipse a flood a quarter inch at a time. I am saying here, that if I pretend I can remember much of anything, I like to think I could see my face in the shot glass. Self as parenthetical, self as wound framed by the less tarnished. I did this to myself, surrounded by my friends who are all prettier than me. Now, too drunk. Now, gone. Now, faded; life span of a bruise.

I wanted that, a reckless beauty; dauntless and inundating the room. I inflict myself on myself. Still. Hasty *yes* and *yes* and *yes*. I thought, even when surrounded, that I was alone. What is there really to learn from Troy, besides isolation begets permeability?

Sacrifice begets visibility; I am never more dazzling than when I'm sucking my own knife clean. I sprinted towards the light, nobody knew I was absent. Past that, desire begets a gash in the memory. I remember teeth, and how the blood didn't leave my neck. Pooled instead. Bruised constellation. Botched hanging. Loud islands of regret. Too drunk. I make terrible prey. Mutter yes as if it can mean anything.

Oh teeth, my one clean memory, little disorganized search lamps, I count you as my audience; the way stars are beautiful until they are revealed as planes; the way what is touched erodes into an unremarkable darkness; the way the light of what is gone; reaches dim, reaches still.

FRANK OCEAN SIGHTING #268: FRANK OCEAN IS RUMORED TO SPEAK OF RIVERS WHICH IS LIKELY A LIE (DISC 1)

Junior year come around
& in my dorm room
animal level desire makes me
more me   in some ways
My savage tongue drizzles
onto an empty bed
Empty   except me
    nothing new
to splinter the obese quiet
Lonely & holding court with stains
Drake vibrates through the next wall

lust got loose in the hallway
sex echoes between melodies
I thumb at flakes of paint
I ain't got nobody   no music
No woman   no man
this makes me the anomaly
again   My man handsome
as anything that don't quite exist
My man just the hum glazing my fist
Beneath my nails   olive coats of landscape

Gossip tells us there's two discs
Rumor tells us it's posthumous
Sense should've told me not to sleep
with this white girl   knowing history
like I do   yet here   me frightened
me jutting my hips in the dull light
Gossip tells us one of the discs

is River   Booze shuffled off her lips
It never met my mouth   I quivered inside her
loneliness   she told me   *You need to quit being*
such uh bitch & fuck me   I obeyed   then exited

For weeks it goes like that
this memory I shudder to call
abuse   Yet it was
the story is gauze
I already bled through it
She called me a coward
for each of my refusals
I ask myself   why I stayed
The sex was bad   I was scared
of her solitude   her fragile quiet
her desire for me to be hers outside
Some vases shatter   get filled with gold
Some vases shatter   just become fractures
that hold my eyes   as I drop the lid over them
Leave their little trauma in the hallway

My whole body an Achilles Heel
momma's ever tender failing
destined for a puncture's fame
The album was a hoax
I was just as depressed as before
& now mother to half a secret
Still I was ablaze with want
for sex   yes   but mostly
I just wanted it to end

My friends & their partners
are in the main room playing Monopoly
discussing gains & losses & losses
I'm invited as an afterthought
Still ablaze I put on my coat
It is 3am   and the downpour is torrential
I shouldn't be going anywhere
I'm not sure I'm going anywhere
so much as testing if anyone would stop me
while I stroll past them   They didn't
& when I stepped outside to quench
the gene which gives me my father's sadness
it rained until every puddle was rabid

NARCISSUS ~~IMPOSTOR SYNDROME~~

Vanity is a sin   but
look what happened
in its absence   maybe it is hard to
leave because I have never
had a face before   less
a question of beauty
than what it is to be unworthy
of even the smallest touch
Maybe every myth is stuck
with thirst   to see a stranger
and never be as much a stranger
again   part of me is always at a lake
that I was not invited to
so when I see anything   I thirst
Once   a boy with insistent hands
touched me in a dark so complete
I lost my own face for months
I couldn't cum   and wouldn't
speak   thus drought   thus I
would rather drown   I would
rather be misinterpreted as loving
myself so much   I die only for me
Only when I drown am I enough
On any land   I fear I am a fraud
I pledge allegiance   only to what
is upfront about wanting me dead
I pledge allegiance to me   sometimes
But I am afraid even of the water
Stupid boy   planned his own death
so poorly   he survived

THE AUTHOR IS OFTEN MISTAKEN FOR OBAMA'S LONG LOST SON

All over the news it is said
He is once in a generation
I understand this to mean
there can only be one of us
and he already is   and often
things are lost for a reason
Me and all my margin heavy
blood-loose a pack of scarlet
hounds howling at the edge of
acceptable   I want to be
what he is but I'm just barely
over the fact I can be seen at all
and the resemblance is marginal
a question of the right brilliance
a question of the hypothetical
a question of *If I had a son he would*
probably not look like me either
The only math I'm good at is counting
what ain't mine   My tongue
   My hands   Faces that can be traded
for other things I can't have   The good
silver creeping at the edge of my scalp
I steady plot the course of history
by the lengths of presidencies
sundial dictating a shadow
All I can remember about time
is what man wanted me dead then
I hear *the 80's* and a hand ribboned
with blue veins raptures the choir

of hair running the length of my calves
Supple meat gone sour in the freezer
Infertile country   Lousy with stray mutts
My fugitive reflection dirtying the anthem
You look just like him   so clean   so smart
It's Midnight in _____   In this light
he could be your father   Where your peoples
from   Yall might have split a ghost way back
Just the spitting image   like that poor boy
The Night makes cousins of us all

INSOMNIAC SOLILOQUY

A Double Golden Shovel

Death might as well be my father's pen name   indecent hours ragged on his breath   and   I
of course am his for knowing the night is no place for the softness even of an eye   I'm never
cousin to the dull hex of my need to guzzle a poor light   by midnight I'm the need itself   Sleep
the property of disembodied birds cooing as if dawn isn't a mocking excuse for free   Because
is this not always the year of two boys fumbling at the other's mortality?   My father says *sleep*
sleep and coins spill onto my eyes   My palms wreak of copper   The reason that I don't sleep is
because he is still so alive   I don't want to miss a single bloodshot eye before I can't forget the
sleep that lasts all my life   I'm asking the night for a drought the diameter of an iris   For *cousin*
never to mean *dead*   O sleep   O father   Are we the children of what we deny ourselves of?
I slept well on his chest and all night his same drab arithmetic: Exhale   Count the gaps in death

MY FATHER WATCHES FERGUSON VOL. 1

I tried to give you religion
on the South Side
but you never been
into glass houses

Honestly I wasn't fussed
God is something
St. Louis never gave me

All I know is winter
and construction and retreat
a relentless swallow
we call a city

This shit?
this ain't nothing new to me
You've met my friends
shaken their scorched fingers

Shoot   once a cop
rolled up next to us
pulled the trigger
on an empty gun
his laugh was a fog

You see how thick they went and made the sky?
that's the religion I know
a heaven low enough to choke on
a god that bring tears to your eyes
just to take back his salt

I don't do much praying
outside counting
how much you don't look like me

I don't ask much of you
but for your mother's sake
don't fuck around
and end up a fable

PORTRAIT OF MY FATHER AS SISYPHUS

Sisyphus always sees the boulder

                                        coming towards him

                                        so each day is like its predecessor

My grandmother lives in Saint Louis   she has never known anywhere else

                                                              I know this

            of the many people

                                    my father   ~~has threatened to kill~~

                                                        been forced to grieve

                        She is never among the dead

            Every two weeks or so   she calls   serrated with confusion

says he is stealing from her   says he has never been any good   says he took the
    money

                the money is in the same place   my father in the same place

pacing the living room   slapping at his thigh   penance for the crime of being

                                                        a good son

                the subtext is that: THE THIEF MUST DIE

what is stolen is almost always irrelevant comparative to the audacity
of the survival itself

            every other week she calls the son   her last son   her only son

my Sisyphus sees the caller ID light up

                        he sees the boulder
                        but cannot turn away

                                            I'm sure he could kill her
                                            by sending it to voicemail

He never does
he returns to the city   that he hates   to reach below the bed

                                                        to play the good son
Now it is August again   and again   and again   he presses himself against her
                The immovable weight of age
                        I watch him drive through the ridges of his own palms
Sisyphus' subtext is: ~~THE THIEF MUST DIE~~

                    LOVE IS A DEATH UNTO ITSELF
        You think Sisyphus did not learn to love the boulder?
What else do you give the love
                        that flays
                                the soft from your palms?
On the TV   mere miles from my grandmother   a good son dies   it is too much
    to ask

                                                her to remember
A combination of a bullet and history cleaves his skull to fragments
            something about Athena would confuse the metaphor here
                            I am grieving a stranger now
                                    and perhaps always
            The subtext is: THE THIEF MUST DIE
        And in the midst of that my father watches   his ugly home contort in
            the smoke
reminisces with my grandmother *Them folk are at it again* and she tells a story
        about some not-Him she caught stealing and he got beat by the whole
            neighborhood
                    the myth is almost sweet in its brutality
But then   of course   the boulder

She forgets he stole nothing until I am on the phone   my name honeying the palms
  she swings

                                                                at my father's memory

Every time after these calls my father sits on the balcony pulling from his E-cigarette
  shucking death from a small halo   calls to me   Sisyphean with exhaustion

Before that happens, kill me. I would rather die than ~~become her~~ haunt you like that.

I know this draft of him well   I too see the boulder coming   he will never kill her
inheritance is a knife   a dull repentance in my palm   the subtext is:
  THE THIEF MUST DIE

MY FATHER WATCHES FERGUSON VOL. 2

I saw something like this before
the eclipse I mean
broad daylight   disappearing

You know how the night hums?
not with god or the remnants
of a siren   just a choir in the dark?
Out here we call those cicadas

Well every so often
bodies come up out the ground
thousands swallow the whole damn sun
that shit   that shit was biblical

But I guess that's not the rebirth
you were looking for
maybe you wanted the one
where the sky disappears entirely
where the sinners march out the city
where salt is the punishment for nostalgia

Sorry about that
this is the only story I know
where winter comes calling
and it start raining corpses
and nobody gets ornery about it

All this shit is cyclical
The cicadas know
they put their children straight
in the ground   command the body
                    "dig"

Now y'all fussed
because they said
He was no angel
Mad they left him in the sun
Left him to dream of shade
while he rot in the heat   turn a country to salt
You can be mad   but you shouldn't be shocked
you know how I feel about looking back

PALINOPSIA

I remember it best as this: the room was all walls; the grief, an impossible architecture. I didn't want to leave the room. I didn't want to leave the room despite having not eaten, I didn't want to step into February. I didn't want to leave the room, even though the room was not mine. It was a dorm room, beige territory, flickering bulb, the paint a fractured cartography. It seemed as if there was nowhere that death was not a question of auto-play. Give me anonymity before that kind of purgatory. It was a good day then if I could tell you how long I had had on the same sweats. Even in the memory the ending seems obvious, I am going to fail out of college. At the time this seemed inconsequential, I was going to die anyway. You have to understand; everyday someone was leaving, I blinked and the copper levitated out of the skull, back to the barrel. It's striking in retrospect, the places we seem to find ourselves before the inevitable. A gun knows its purpose; I envy that, still. Several flies hovered trying to force themselves into the bulb. This is how I know I would make for a poor god, I didn't have the energy to kill them myself though I wanted to. Instead, I would go back to sleep, summon the energy to turn off the light, I shut down their heaven once it began to inconvenience me. Next to the stream of the people like me dying there were emails that read "Checking in," "Absences," "Graduation?" But the videos were all connected, an electric rosary, every new saint stained an iris. I say that the room was all walls, but there was also a window, the window doesn't mean hope, it means I can't be trusted with my own erosion. I say the room was all walls to mean: Every door is an obligation. My father's calls went unanswered. The emails went unanswered. The body went undiagnosed. All of these are my fault. I didn't want a diagnosis, I had a country already. I didn't want a diagnosis, because I am convinced a name is something incurable. The letter that told me I was not going to graduate used the phrase "Regrets" 8 times. Outside the window I forget about, the suburb was thawing. The blinds made a beggar of the light, while I started a panic attack; behind my eyelids: February and February and February.

POLICE DREAM #607

Analyze my demise I say I'm super anxious
■ KENDRICK LAMAR ■

A fog of mosquitos collides around
the last of the streetlights
Drunk on the idea of a false heaven
a dying moon to bask in

The feeble glow
a second hand god
his own silver moon
shining in his chest
My mother's pulse aching in time
with my blood's boastful song
He raises his hand
a country of twitching rivers
fat blue veins sculpting his knuckles
Ashes mark me holy

The shadows of the mosquitos
swell as they flee the streetlight
I become a borderless land
riddled with tiny red rebellions
        a slow eclipse
I breathe in the last dregs of summer
then the flood of small thieves
christen me harvest with their greedy mouths

The organ sinks its hundred blunt teeth into
each mourning song

Elders bow their heads
faces   a cartography
of what was survived

PALINOPSIA

I remember it best as this: **the room was** all walls; the **grief,** an impossible
architecture. I didn't want to leave the room. I didn't want to leave the
room despite having not eaten, I didn't want to step into February. I
didn't want to leave the room, even though the room was not mine. It
was **a** dorm room, beige territory, flickering bulb, the paint a fractured
cartography. It seemed as if there was nowhere that death was not a
question of auto-play. Give me anonymity before that kind **of purgatory.**
It was a good day then if I could tell you how long I had had on the same
sweats. Even in the memory the ending **seems obvious,** I am going to
fail out of college. At the time this seemed inconsequential, I was going
to die anyway. You have to understand; **everyday** someone was leaving,
I blinked and the copper **levitated** out of the skull, **back to the barrel.**
It's striking in **retrospect,** the places we seem to find ourselves before
the inevitable. A gun knows its purpose; **I envy** that, still. **Several flies**
hovered trying to force themselves into **the bulb.** This is how **I know**
I would make for a poor god, **I didn't have the energy to kill** them
myself though I wanted to. Instead, I would go back to sleep, summon
the energy to turn off the light, I shut down their heaven once it began
to inconvenience me. Next to the stream of the people like me dying
there were emails that read "Checking in," **"Absences,"** "Graduation?"
But the videos were all **connected,** an electric rosary, **every new saint**
stained an iris. I say that the room was all walls, but there was also a
window, the window doesn't mean hope, it means I can't be trusted
with my own **erosion.** I say the room was all walls to mean: Every
door **is an obligation. My** father's calls went unanswered. The emails
went unanswered. The **body went undiagnosed.** All of these are **my**
fault. I didn't want a diagnosis, I had a country already. I didn't want a
diagnosis, because I am convinced a **name is something incurable.** The
letter that told me I was not going to graduate used the phrase "Regrets"
8 times. Outside the window I forget about, the suburb was thawing. The
blinds made a beggar of the light, while I started a panic attack; behind
my eyelids: February and February and February.

ELEGY FOR THE SUMMER AFTER
DJANGO UNCHAINED CAME OUT ON DVD

Is it really love if there's not a burning house behind you?
July left me the smoke trickling into the unquenchable

I watched Django eight times in a single summer
Before   I didn't know burgundy was my color
I didn't want the wound to forget it was a wound

so I watered it with salt
I am too depressed to stay the uppity beast

If I break the hand that starves me
what would I do with the other?

my chest   the muzzled orchestra   whistling rusted hinges
Is it really love if there's not a burning house behind you?

I watered it with salt
gore leaves the men like silk
tapestries   a lineage   100 black coffins

the shade of my father's hair   The same greying fever
undiagnosed   a scalding yoke   *the D is silent*   the name
inescapable

PALINOPSIA

I remember it best as this: the room was all walls; the grief, an impossible architecture. I didn't want to leave the room. I didn't want to leave the room despite having not eaten, I didn't want to step into February. I didn't want to leave the room, even though the room was not mine. It was a dorm room, beige territory, flickering bulb, the paint a fractured cartography. It seemed as if there was nowhere that death was not a question of auto-play. Give me anonymity before that kind of purgatory. It was a good day then if I could tell you how long I had had on the same sweats. Even in the memory the ending seems obvious, I am going to fail out of college. At the time this seemed inconsequential, I was going to die anyway. You have to understand; everyday someone was leaving, I blinked and the copper levitated out of the skull, back to the barrel. It's striking in retrospect, the places we seem to find ourselves before the inevitable. A gun knows its purpose; I envy that, still. Several flies hovered trying to force themselves into the bulb. This is how I know I would make for a poor god, I didn't have the energy to kill them myself though I wanted to. Instead, I would go back to sleep, summon the energy to turn off the light, I shut down their heaven once it began to inconvenience me. Next to the stream of the people like me dying there were emails that read "Checking in," "Absences," "Graduation?" But the videos were all connected, an electric rosary, every new saint stained an iris. I say that the room was all walls, but there was also a window, the window doesn't mean hope, it means I can't be trusted with my own erosion. I say the room was all walls to mean: Every door is an obligation. My father's calls went unanswered. The emails went unanswered. The body went undiagnosed. All of these are my fault. I didn't want a diagnosis, I had a country already. I didn't want a diagnosis, because I am convinced a name is something incurable. The letter that told me I was not going to graduate used the phrase "Regrets" 8 times. Outside the window I forget about, the suburb was thawing. The blinds made a beggar of the light, while I started a panic attack; behind my eyelids: February and February and February.

REGRETS

Student
Senior at _____College
May 2015

Dear Mr. _____,

It is with great regret that we must announce that the Committee on Academic Affairs has judged that you be required to withdraw from school for the coming year. This will, of course, mean that you will not graduate with your class. We are sorry to see this inconvenience of your skin come to pass. Unfortunately, your petition regarding your "Inability to sleep due to persistent taste of dirt," the "dysphoria of lungs, still functioning" and "sudden, violent panic attacks due to images of Black death" are not under the college's list of approved reasons for absence. We remind you, again, that many seniors have concerns about their futures and still managed to attend and pass all their classes.

Regarding the reapplication process we find it is often best for students to take some time to relax and reassess whether this institution is a good fit for them going forward. While it is unlikely that you have not already considered this, we feel it best to remind students who have gone astray. Though we have no official records of your slow erosion, it has been evident in your grades over the course of your time here. We hope that you know that we want you to succeed here.

Finally, we must inform you that a copy of this letter and your many failures will be sent to your parents/guardians. Given that you are a senior you will no longer be eligible for financial aid on your courses. Any attempts to petition for funding will be returned unread. We understand that your parents "have sacrificed everything for you" to be here. We understand they will likely "never retire as a result." We truly regret that your mother's hands will "ruin themselves with prayer and office work." It is always hard for us to deliver this news to any family. We hope that you can take this time to have a dialogue with them about how everything was for you, how everything was for nothing.

We look forward to your potential return and wish you the best going forward.

Sincerely,
The Committee on Academic Affairs

GHAZAL FOR THE SUICIDAL THOUGHT

I ask the therapist *How long do you have to think about suicide*
before you can actually say for certain that the thought is suicide

and not just a desire to fly long enough to be anywhere else?
She seems stumped   asks again   *Well have you thought of suicide?*

Almost all my favorite songs end in the sound of a gunshot
almost all my waking thoughts are music   melody caught in suicide

But I have never thought of ending it   not that way   Only a cop
would be able to stare into my mother and say: *Accident* mean: *Suicide*

My mother asks me over the dinner table something that is not a question
my quiet is a static veil over her face   *I worry: Is he going to commit suicide*

The not-question swells to the circumference of the iris of a pistol
I dream of windows when I feel out of place   am I always thinking of suicide?

Maybe not   maybe I just don't know what I would be if I wasn't tragic
but there was a time   Mid-June   a train whistle   sound wrought suicide

I am the worst thing that has ever happened to this family Who would notice
another Black boy obliterated by metal?   If it looks like an accident is it suicide?

I failed out of college   that same day   every sacrifice coating my skull
a bassline begging for a gunshot   some great songs end in suicide

I didn't jump   I didn't jump   I didn't jump   I am sorry   I rode the bullet
train home like Icarus rode his father's work into the sea   Is ambition a suicide?

Still I have my other forms of suicide   the unavoidable sin   of Checkers
    insomnia   my lust   my house   how fast the train   how slow the suicide

PALINOPSIA

I remember it best as this: the room was all walls; the grief, an impossible architecture. I didn't want to leave the room. I didn't want to leave the room despite having not eaten, I didn't want to step into February. I didn't want to leave the room, even though the room was not mine. It was a dorm room, beige territory, flickering bulb, the paint a fractured cartography. It seemed as if there was nowhere that death was not a question of auto-play. Give me anonymity before that kind of purgatory. It was a good day then **if I** could **tell you** how long I had had on the same sweats. Even in the memory the ending seems obvious, **I am going to fail out of college**. At the time this seemed inconsequential, I was going to die anyway. **You have to understand**; everyday **someone was leaving**, I blinked and the copper levitated out of the skull, back to the barrel. It's striking in retrospect, the places we seem to find ourselves before the inevitable. A gun knows its purpose; **I envy that, still.** Several flies hovered trying to force themselves into the bulb. This is how I know I would make for a poor god, I didn't have the energy to kill them myself though I wanted to. Instead, I would go back to sleep, summon the energy to turn off the light, I shut down their heaven once it began to inconvenience me. Next to the stream of the people like me dying there were emails that read "Checking in," "Absences," "**Graduation?**" But the videos were all connected, an electric rosary, every new saint stained an iris. I say that the room was all walls, but there was also a window, the window **doesn't mean hope, it means I can't be trusted** with my own erosion. I say the room was all walls to mean: Every door is an obligation. My father's calls went unanswered. **The** emails went unanswered. The body went undiagnosed. All of these are my **fault**. I didn't want a diagnosis, I had **a country** already. **I didn't want** a diagnosis, because I am convinced a name is something incurable. The letter that told me I was not going to graduate used the phrase "Regrets" 8 times. Outside the window I forget about, the suburb was thawing. The blinds made a beggar of the light, while I started a panic attack; behind my eyelids: February and February and February.

THE SEARCH FOR FRANK OCEAN OR
A BRIEF HISTORY OF DISAPPEARING

Fucking pig get shot, 300 men will search for me
■ FRANK OCEAN ■

A drought does not name itself
in anything but the splintering
of skin into a series of wanting
rivers and the cities that gave
all that water a name as if it
were kin   as if July were not
    slow piano and crimson
all over the street   and I guess
you could call this a war
in the way only who can be seen
is alive and maybe not even that

    .

August prepares its heavy gown
for our shoulders and I have
nothing to sing   but the heat
on the screen   two trends
#BatonRougePolice
        #WheresTheAlbumFrank

    .

Happy June 222nd
    Happy anniversary Frank
        Maybe Frank was never even there
This album definitely not done
        Frank need to come home
    This gay ass nigga gonna break our hearts again

All I want is a song
                              This nigga a lie
                He fix his mouth   and nothing spills out
Frank might be dead y'all
                              Frank might be dead y'all
        Another nigga gone missing
                        Happy June 225th
                                        I swear he never coming back
I swear I saw him
                        I swear it's been Summer for 3 years

                .

A name is something you surrender
in parts   if you are lucky
        I am not
much more beyond that
which traces the borders of me
into a bed in mid-July
        I am not
much more than my secrets

                .

Boy say Bi_____
and his tongue splits

Boy say Bi_____
and his mouth is public property

Boy say Bi_____
and belongs nowhere

Boy say Bi_____
and now none of his gods
return his calls

.

A body gets silent
and it is either haunted
or will be

A body gets silent
and everyone can sing it dead

A body gets silent
and is named after the silence
to forget it was ever a boy

Silence inundates my throat
there is more than one way
to have a boy in your mouth

.

The body is a glass home
I am somewhere   I used to live
fragile and nearly translucent
opaque only where smoke tongues
me into the illusion of shelter
I shatter/into more/me

VARIATION ON A THEME OF GENETICS

After Kendrick Lamar

In the dregs of August I watch the birds sprint like Black folk   and surely this
    is in my DNA
the loudness of living amongst the living breaks one bird loose into armada
    of wings in my DNA

Where I'm from is a question I can only answer in my parents' capillaries and
    thus I know only a bruise's worth of my origin
I have 1 country and 1 executioner   they're the same in my DNA

Tradition dictates the men in my family die of nothing but themselves   and so
    I am a fugitive
percussion   child of bad knees   I sprint an emaciated hum until I'm a threat
    to my DNA

Beneath my skin I keep 23 versions of the same drowned map   I am a library
    of redundancies
bird lost amongst birds   I was built in and for obscurity   all the darkness is
    practical in my DNA

The body is a subtle phalanx   by which I mean   I am never not thinking
    about dying
Every child being born is also being sent to their death   I calculate the mercies
    in my DNA

each night as if I could bend pinion into a frail sickle   slake every thirsting
    palm with a blade
There's a joke that nothing makes Black people run faster   than
    other Black people running

Tell me something
                    only if you know it
Why are we running   if not because the loyalty is in our DNA   native as an
    apocalypse
                    Do the birds know
                                        their blades look like blades against

even a threatless sky
                            what is patience
                            but a luxury of the hunted

the appeasement of a mosquito is just a docile format of bloodshed   tell me

                                        when destruction gonna be our fate
                            surrender is as expensive as it is unjustifiable

                    I am trying to vanquish a hereditary sadness

I am trying to say I was born with my mother's face
                    and my father's skin who says   I have the face of the future
                named so   for being the last obscurity   he will see before he dies
just my luck   to be born   a few years before
                                                    the end of the world
my parents draw nearer the end of their running   we are listening
        for the tragedy that will escort them out of this life   leaving me
    holding only the blood

LESLIE ODOM JR. SINGS OBAMA'S ANGER ON NPR

The strings twitch into a song
the way the wind flinches a tree
into the end of October
I look into   the belly of Mississippi
and on screen the Black man opens
his mouth to reveal a small white woman
and the song is a fugitive just like that
the song is a mask made of everyone
I have ever loved   and all the quiet
we are now   The song is and is and is
and ends   A hair exhausted of its color
gone now to the shade of harp strings which
beckons the fingers to harm themselves
into a music   and I imagine hatred
must require an entire orchestra
A legion of calloused working hands
similar to my Father's own pair
only in the weight and desire
But again what else is there to a pair of hands
besides what can be flayed loose?
Beneath the skin perhaps a matrix of bones
sun starved and maybe even the color of mercy
Maybe not   maybe just a barely country
maybe the most fathomable wound
And this is less about anger than it is drought
how dehydration is considered a failure
of the well   rather than an impeachment
upon the throat   And here it is as hot as ever
Here a November where nothing is cold enough
to die   Here Obama's anger Chechen dolls onto
my computer and everything a man hasn't said
lays a bloody lullaby in my lap and this too is history
a labor of callouses and blisters and other casualties

of running and I have never known music not to escape
I have never known myself not a fugitive from my own anger
I have never known us not sprinting as if sung from somewhere else
And in the distance men send bullets into the sky and sing hallelujah
and their song is the unstitching of a scab   and maybe I look out the window
and mistake the copper for a star   maybe I mistake the violence   for home

MERCY, MERCY, HIM

The first time I realized Marvin Gaye was dead
was the first time I realized my father wasn't joking
when he said   *I could kill you*

Please   forgive him
for what he believes his rage demands
forgive him   as I have failed to

I know Marvin like I know my father
gazing up in half laughter   venom in the breeze
if I must die   and I must   let him be the gun

A death is only like a firework
in how it can become a mistake
in the space between rooms

When Marvin died   his brother blamed fireworks
a man can die from how his country celebrates
a man can die from another man

When he wrapped his hands around my throat
I wore his callouses like pearls   threw the second punch
asked no mercy   except *God spare the man who is killing me*

Forgive me   I had forgotten it was the beginning of July
my vision populated with false stars
what could be misremembered   as fireworks

TANKA FOR THE 4TH OF JULY

I will spend the day
surviving which is the most
un-American
use of my body since I
spat loose a bullet and laughed

ZEALOTS OF STOCKHOLM OR ELEGY FOR THE STILL ALIVE

After Childish Gambino

I. MY FATHER SAYS GOODBYE AGAIN AND AGAIN

I miss your grandfather he taught me how to say goodbye
by never saying it   every dawn brings a cardinal   his wings splay goodbye

He showed up at my Junior year dorm with a six pack
already gone   he was dying   never told me   by that May   goodbye

What did I know then about leaving besides the smoke
I could chuckle out? What did I know of gone outside my own gray goodbye?

In the dreams he is still buried   sometimes he is a dragonfly
fragments of light pierce the little cathedral of his wings in each ray a goodbye

The night you were born   a cardinal landed on the windowsill
feeble resurrection under a blue moon   his red feathers a bouquet of goodbye

Never let me haunt you   nobody you've known was built to stay
burn me   take me anywhere but St. Louis   let the ash spray goodbye

All I need in this life is to see you further than he saw me get Your spine
ran the length of my palm once   little rosary   I pray you get to say goodbye

II. MOURNING MY NOT-DEAD FATHER

For my father's sake I say goodbye whenever I leave the room. The ghost is just a prop, the weight is theoretical and everywhere. My father has always spoken of himself as though the kiln moans only for him. I'm a stenographer of elegies for the still living; this is an unremarkable fact because everyone has an inheritance. There's a theory where only what is visible is in fact alive; until that you're dead. Now I am far from my father & what is there to say he is alive besides my mother? My mother who never leaves my father's side. My mother who I am far from too. My mother who my father says will live forever. My mother who will not tell my Abuelo that he has cancer for fear it will upset him. My mother who will never retire because of what it has cost to keep me alive. My mother who loves her son who failed out of college. My mother who always calls. My mother who didn't call to tell me my tio had been dead for a week so I wouldn't fail all my classes again. My mother who loves me enough to keep me in the dark. My mother who wants simple things; pajamas, my father's laugh, a son who remembers the scar he came from, men who speak as though they will live forever. My mother who wants to spare us; a vase full only with the living. My mother who I used to pick flowers for from the sidewalks, little dented things I saved from underfoot. This too is inheritance, these mercies that were not mine to give.

III. THE INEVITABLE URN

He is still alive
so I hadn't considered
the necessity of the urn
its design   its unimaginable
weight will someday be him
I would pick a charcoal glazed
until my own face distorts on
his new surface as it does in life
I have my mother's face her mercy
but these are no doubt   his eyes
that I will one-day shield
as I let the breeze take him

OBAMA WANTS TO BE CLEAR ABOUT HIS LEGACY

Let me be clear   as a water stain
on glass   nearly window but not
bulletproof   I want some things
to always be constant   Legacy
is muzzled by history with good
reason   Let me be clearer still
a persistent film of dew on dying
grass   Opacity is a form of treason
I gut envelopes with a thin gold
and sometimes my own dead face
unspools and men in suits rush in
because it would be a tragedy
if I remembered I was someone
who could die   Let me be clear
my blood necessitates repetition
I am gone   I am gone I am gone
I am grateful that the room was
round or I would have dented it
with my screams   Gratitude
is a kind of violence   I say *thank
you* and that yawns into a bomb
Everything I do I do with a grace
which has only ever been described
as bestial   A gazelle or a swan
I'm a precise kind of fugitive
When I was born   history stuttered
I lacquer my palms with the silence
I think it's impossible not to miss it
Despite everything I give white people hope
Nothing will ever demand me to be
this merciless   again

OBAMA SPEAKS OF RIVERS BUT WE HAVE ALWAYS BEEN ON DIFFERENT SHORES

If it is true that a people can be a river then me and my
father wore the good shoes   just to stand at the bank Soul
music washed up from the speakers in Springfield Obama has
gathered us here   fulfilling a promise   three years grown
I'm in 8th grade   it is 2007   I'm a little country in a little country deep
in the midst of wars   as in plural as in the skies here are blue like
they cannot be wherever men drop bombs to get rich   The
speech is about to start   folk have come from all over like rivers

We rode the bus up from Chicago in February at 5 in the morning
in dress clothes as if he would be able to see us amid all that hope
We rode the bus full of folk who looked nothing like us to go cheer
a man   who looked like us   though the resemblance stopped

at a mutual inability to burn under the weightless pressure of a gaze
We are in the crowd   at the radius of visible   and I know his arrival
only by the holler of taller people   I can't see anything that isn't above me
t-shirts banged loose from the cannon   fast clouds punctuating the sky

It's cold enough that I forget the speech worrying at my numbing toes
even if I were tall   I will never be close enough   to see the breath escape him
in little pearl colored gusts   beneath my feet not a stage but cobblestones
some still full with little muddy rivers of snow   yes   I've known rivers

I have stood abreast of them leaning against my father's good coat
Kid leather full to the brim with what makes a goose eligible to float
against the heady sky   This coat he used to carry me inside as a baby
this womb he was given by my mother   this thing he shed as a gift to me

later that same year   This little bet he made   with himself that I would
Grow into it   that he loved my mother who stayed in Omaha
selling the last great thing we owned so she could come home
that his feet must have been cold too that day   We had even worn dress socks

thin fabric to a party we not even on the waiting list to the waiting list for
thin fabric inside the shoes that he would loan me to wear to my first prom
thin fabric abreast of a little series of embankments   shores between the wind
Yes   I've known rivers   my father and I straddled them below Lincoln's face

I've stood abreast of this river within a river of onlookers
I've stood and not drowned
My father places his arm around me to keep warm
crouches at his overworked knees   *Can you see him son?*
And beneath my little hat   part of his voice is lost in the skin
I say   *No*   and watch his face crease
He becomes the bed of the Mississippi

He reaches beneath my armpits his palms matching small valleys I am 110 pounds
There   the brief inhale before he tries to lift me to his shoulders   above him
as he always planned   We both know I am too big to lift O my father
my Sisyphus   I return to the earth
knowing now that my father loves me to failure

and yet   he returned to the work of showing me who I could be   My
father bent again within inches of prayer on the frozen street while the soul
of the country contemplated whether it was ready to lift a man who has
no father left to lift him just to see a brown spot   I thought I was too grown
to see   The second time   he lifts me   I sit on his shoulders falling deep

in love with this man whose blood is not my blood who people say I am like
But I thought then   *Maybe this country is mine*   On the
bus ride back   we sang   amidst white folk   We sang past the rivers

NEGROTOPIA #3 (SELF PORTRAIT AS HEAVEN)

We like the promised land of the OGs
■ KANYE WEST ■

Cue the Anthony Hamilton/and name me a mansion/tell everyone there is
space here/if you believe in the reincarnated/I am already somewhere/that
somebody has gone/after they died/so I am heaven/cue the gold clouds/the
gospel songs/the voices you didn't know you missed/until you heard them/for
the first time/watch me glitter/watch me gold/watch me be exactly the show
you were promised/forget what tried to kill you/just for a second/forget its
name/and only remember that it missed/cue the wings/cue the rain/I promise
this is not the end/I promise we get to be everywhere now/I promise that
the only heaven/that can hold us/is us

SAD NIGGA MANIFESTO

After Terrance Hayes

*I won't blunt my blade for cut these chains /
rather let my limbs be drug through the mud*
■ **FRANK OCEAN** ■

Some songs can only be the orange echo
of a Western sky   Something is always spilling
and the heat mops it up before the stain
even has a chance to name itself
I was born exhausted of fleeing
I am coming to you live from
a Negro spiritual born with dust in its veins
and little else   Melody of heat lightning
threading the space between desert and stars
Let's say what's real   I'm a sad nigga
come from a long line of sad niggas
I am coming to you live from a generation
of thirst   Everyone I know is trying to fit their calluses
around the throat of grief   It seems like it has come to this
it seems like it has only ever been this
What is abandoned in trying to leave sadness
as if it is the lonely opera of a day lit storm?   My family
I am coming to you live from straddling a noteless tragedy
I am wandering through a harmony built from bloodlines
and humidity and the tenderness only fugitives can claim
It took a precise sequence of sins to make me
and I am giving none of them back

Only a mouth can cure a mouth   A man is singing
in the distance   and he too is a sad nigga come from
a lineage of the unforgiven   I want to find him
I want to manifest destiny my own sadness
Thirst to shining thirst   shame to shining shame
If I find him   we will hum as if we are bullets
discovering the labor of bullets   heat lightning
unspooling amethyst   until death do I part
from the life I have tarnished with my living

ACKNOWLEDGMENTS

Versions of these poems appeared in the following publications:

Acentos Review, Adroit Journal, Anomaly Magazine, Bird's Thumb, Big Lucks, BOAAT, Callaloo, Emerge Literary Journal, HEArt Journal, Hermeneutic Chaos Journal, Indiana Review, The Journal, Kweli, Michigan Quarterly Review, Misrepresented Peoples Anthology, Nashville Review, New York Times Magazine, Prairie Schooner, Puerto del Sol, Queen's Mob Teahouse, Rattle, The Rumpus, Shade Journal, Sixth Finch, Sundog Lit, Up the Staircase Quarterly, Word Riot, and *Wusgood Black*

I find myself with the impossible task of expressing my gratitude to everyone who has made this book possible. Above all others I have to thank my parents, my ever present champions who never wavered in teaching me that I could do anything; my mother who taught me how to be a friend and my father who taught me how to read and in so doing taught me to fly. I want to thank my Sister for being a constant friend and showing me how to hold myself with pride wherever I went, my nephew Dominic for teaching me from the moment of his birth how to fight and how to love as well.

I want to thank my brilliant siblings (for we are a family even if our blood is not the same) in this work without whom I would have countless times been lost to the world, without whom this book would not, could not exist. Noel, when I call you Natiao it means that English has given me no word for this kind of love, thank you always for saying yes to being my family, for holding my hand when the dark crept in. George, I have said a thousand times and will say a thousand more that I do not know what I did in a past life to deserve someone as kind and brave and fiercely loving as you to be my best friend, thank you for challenging me everyday to be a better me. Jayson, it is one thing to owe someone your life, it is something else entirely to owe them several of your lives, how could I have known that on a muggy August day in New York in the worst summer I had ever endured that my life was already beginning to change, as you once said to me at Callaloo, thank you for making me brave. Nick, my faith has always been a fickle thing but I have no greater proof of God than that we have found each other, thank you for never letting me forget who I am. Thank you, all of you, for what you have given in the name of keeping me alive, I am here in no small part because of you.

Every life is built of a lineage of teachers and mentors, I am beyond lucky to have had so many brilliant minds and hearts in my corner. Thank you to Greenie, Mr. Stone, Mr. Fuder, Ms. Dilg, Mr. Moos who dealt with my love for words and lifelong war on punctuation with eyes towards a future I could have never imagined for myself. Thank you Perry "Vision" DiVirgilio who took a sad freshman poet under his wing, every intersection of my poetic life rings with your voice. Thank you Thomas Devaney and Natalie Anderson who watched my first tentative steps toward the page with a warmth I may never again experience. Thank you Diane Anderson who said yes, over and over a Yes I could scarcely whisper to myself. Thank you to Rowan Ricardo Phillips, my predecessor in so many ways, my friend in so many others. There is perhaps no one who has been more instrumental in my work demanding honesty of myself than Greg Pardlo who taught me how to celebrate the superpower and how to write less boring poems. Words cannot describe the joy and luck I feel to be working with Aimee Nezhukumatatil every day, thank you for the gift of your time and making somewhere far from home feel far less so. And boundless gratitude to my big brother, Derrick Harriell who took a tremendous risk to bring me to his table, I can only hope that I can one day make you as proud of me as I am every day to work with you.

I live in awe of and community with a tremendous network of writers who everyday challenge me to push that much harder to be the best I can be. Thank you to Danez Smith, Nate Marshall, Itiola Jones, Natalie Diaz, Gabriel Ramirez, Nkosi Nkululeko, Natasha Trethewey, Paul Tran, Jericho Brown, Kavindu Jointe, Daniella Toosie-Watson, Hanif Abdurraqib, John Murillo, Kirwyn Sutherland, Kiese Laymon, Nadia Alexis, Patricia Smith, Christopher Greggs, Ariana Brown, Cat Velez, Rachel McKibbens, Jose Olivarez, Aziza Barnes, Safia Elhillo, Tara Betts, Ross Gay, Terrance Hayes, Fatimah Asghar, Franny Choi, Sam Sax, Kyle Dargan, Joshua Bennett, Caroline Randall Williams, Nikky Finney, Aracelis Girmay, Malcolm Friend, Jesmyn Ward, Tyriek White, Josh Nguyen, Nicole Terez Dutton, Jess Rizkallah, Melissa Lozada-Oliva, William Evans, Monica Sok, Miriam Harris, Sarah Sgro, Nabila Lovelace, Thiahera Nurse, Erika L. Sanchez, Javier Perez, Luther Hughes, Phillip B. Williams, Evie Shockley, L. Lamar Wilson, Eugenia Leigh, Mahogany L. Browne, Amanda Johnston, Diamond Forde, Kaveh Akbar, Hiwot Adilow, Desiree C. Bailey, Sam Stevens, Justin Phillip Reed, Haydil Henriquez, Hazem Fahmy, Elizabeth Acevedo, Shane McCrae, Jamal Parker, Kendrick Lamar, Soledad Alfaro-Allah, Denice Frohman, Yasmin Belkhyr, Rachel Wiley, Nicole Sealey, Claudia Rankine, Paul Cato, Harmony Holiday, Janelle Viera, Khadijah Queen, Kai Davis, David Pratt, Jovan McKoy, Saeed Jones, Hieu Minh Nguyen, Cortney Lamar Charleston, Jonathan Jacob Moore, Donald Glover, SZA, Ian Axel Anderson, Noor Jaber, Shreekari Tedapali, Sanam Sheriff, Carol Bowe, Xandria Phillips, Jayy Dodd, Audre Lorde, James Baldwin, Kevin Young, Taryn Englehart, Taylor Steele, Camonghne Felix, and Kanye West.

Thank you to the families, spaces and institutions without whom there isn't a book to speak of. Thank you to Cornelius Eady and Toi Derricotte for founding Cave Canem, to Dr. Charles Henry Rowell for founding Callaloo, to Monifa Lemons and Candace Wiley who founded The Watering Hole and introduced me to 4 of my very closest friends until we were kin. Thank you No Name Collective for whom our star has only begun to shine. Thank you to the writers of the BOAAT Retreat and the brilliant family that is the MFA Program at Ole Miss! An unpayable debt to OASIS, my first writing community. If I am clear on nothing else, please know that I owe Philly Youth Poetry Movement nothing less than my life.

Thank you to Ed Ochester and the University of Pittsburgh Press for taking these pages and making a dream come true. And finally, Vievee Francis, how can I find where to begin? Without you I cannot write this book because without you I am not myself. Not the self I needed to be, you have made me brave and knowledgeable beyond my wildest dreams when I first began to write in earnest this project which began as what I imagined would be a last record and turned out to be the seed to an impossible life. Not a day passes that I can look to the work and not ask "What would Vievee do?" To which the answer is always the same, "Work, live, know your craft, be the vanguard you were meant to be." Thank you for saying yes to this book, thank you for giving me the courage to choose this life, the certainty to know it is the only one that I would ever choose.

8/19